Say Cheese

GW00792777

Mr. Frank sat on
the farm gate.

"Take a photo of me,"
he said to Mrs. Frank.

"Say cheese!" said Mrs. Frank.

"Cheese," said Mr. Frank.

But before Mrs. Frank
could take the photo,
a dog came along.

5

"Say cheese!" said Mrs. Frank.

"Cheese," said Mr. Frank.

But before Mrs. Frank
could take the photo,
a sheep came along.

"Say cheese!" said Mrs. Frank.

"Cheese," said Mr. Frank.

But before Mrs. Frank
could take the photo,
a cow came along.

"Say cheese!" said Mrs. Frank.

"Cheese," said Mr. Frank.

But before Mrs. Frank
could take the photo,
a horse came along.

Now there were so many animals, they hid Mr. Frank.

"I can't see you," said Mrs. Frank.

So Mr. Frank stood up.
He started to wobble.

"Quick," he said,
"take the photo!"

"Say cheese!" said Mrs. Frank.